D1263702

Hurricane Katrina and America's Response

A MODERN PERSPECTIVES BOOK

Tamra B. Orr

Published in the United States of America by Cherry Lake Publishing
Ann Arbor, Michigan
www.cherrylakepublishing.com

Content Adviser: Satta Sarmah Hightower, Writer & Editor, Talented Tenth Media, Boston, MA
Reading Adviser: Marla Conn MS, Ed., Literacy specialist, Read-Ability, Inc.

Photo Credits: © Robert A. Mansker / Shutterstock.com, cover, 1; © asiseeit / iStock.com, 4; © joeynick / iStock.com, 5; ©jpbcpa / iStock.com, 7; Ronny Simpson/FEMA, 9; U.S. Navy/Petty Officer 3rd Class Jay C. Pugh/U.S. Department of Defense, 10; U.S. Coast Guard/Petty Officer 2nd Class Kyle Niemi, 11; © Aneese / iStock.com, 12; U.S. Coast Guard/Petty Officer 1st Class Melissa Leake, 14; U.S. Coast Guard, 15; Jocelyn Augustino/FEMA, 17, 20; Marty Bahamonde/FEMA, 19; © Monkey Business Images / Shutterstock.com, 22; Mark Wolfe/FEMA, 23; Ed Edahl/FEMA, 25; Jocelyn Augustino/FEMA, 27; © Terry Poche / Shutterstock.com, 30

Graphic Element Credits: ©RoyStudioEU/Shutterstock.com, back cover, front cover, multiple interior pages; ©queezz/Shutterstock.com, back cover, front cover, multiple interior pages

Library of Congress Cataloging-in-Publication Data
Names: Orr, Tamra B., author.
Title: Hurricane Katrina and America's response / Tamra B. Orr.
Description: Ann Arbor : Cherry Lake Publishing, 2017. | Series: Modern perspectives | Includes
    bibliographical references and index.
Identifiers: LCCN 2016058623| ISBN 9781634728591 (hardcover) | ISBN 9781534100374
    (paperback) | ISBN 9781634729482 (PDF) | ISBN 9781534101265 (hosted ebook)
Subjects: LCSH: Hurricane Katrina, 2005—Social aspects—Louisiana—New Orleans—Juvenile
    literature. | Hurricane Katrina, 2005—Juvenile literature. | New Orleans (La.)—History—21st
    century—Juvenile literature. | New Orleans (La.)—Social conditions—21st century—Juvenile
    literature. | Disaster victims—Louisiana—New Orleans—Biography—Juvenile literature. |
    New Orleans (La.)—Biography—Juvenile literature.
Classification: LCC F379.N557 O77 2017 | DDC 976.3/35—dc23
LC record available at https://lccn.loc.gov/2016058623

Cherry Lake Publishing would like to acknowledge the work of
The Partnership for 21st Century Skills. Please visit www.p21.org
for more information.

Printed in the United States of America
Corporate Graphics

Table of Contents

In this book, you will read three different perspectives about Hurricane Katrina, which struck the coast of United States in late August 2005. While these characters are fictionalized, each perspective is based on real things that happened to real people during and after the hurricane. As you'll see, the same event can look different depending on one's point of view.

Chapter 1

Philip Norris

Storm Survivor

For the 500th time, my thoughts drifted to the glass of iced tea that had been sitting on my desk just a couple of days ago. I could picture the ice cubes in it and the trickles of water condensed on the outside of the glass. What I wouldn't give for that iced tea right now!

"It's so hot!" said my little sister, Lisa. She was right. It had to be over 100 degrees Fahrenheit (38 degrees Celsius) in the attic, and this was our third day stuck inside it.

My mother passed around our last bottle of water, allowing each of us to take a single sip. It was warm, but it still tasted good. I just wish it came with a big sandwich and a pile of chips. We hadn't eaten anything

▲ *The flood waters after Hurricane Katrina rose to 20 feet (6 meters) high in some areas.*

since we ran up here, and our stomachs were grumbling.

"I'm so sorry," my mother muttered. "I should have listened to all of those warnings, but I was just so worried about the animals."

I had heard many of the warnings on television and radio. The weather forecaster had used frightening words such as "devastating damage" and "unprecedented strength" when he talked about the hurricane that was coming. Mayor Nagin had issued the city's first-ever **evacuation** order. Almost everyone I knew had packed up and left New Orleans, but we did not own a car, and Mom didn't want to leave our pets behind.

Lisa gave Mom a hug. "It's okay, Mommy," she whispered. "Help will come soon. Right, Phil?" She looked at me with her big eyes.

Think About It

▶ Read the paragraph about why Philip's family was still in New Orleans. What was the main reason? Give two details that support why you think this.

▲ *Cities and towns in areas that have frequent storms or flooding often have evacuation plans in place in case of an emergency.*

Second Source

▶ Find a second source that describes what happened to the levees in New Orleans. Compare the information there to the information in this chapter.

"You bet!" I said, nodding my head. "One of those helicopters we keep hearing will come to our house any minute."

Even though I didn't believe what I had just said, I wanted to. I was tired, hungry, and very scared. When the storm had hit, I couldn't believe how fast our house filled up with water. Someone outside shouted that one of the **levees** by Lake Pontchartrain had failed. The levees had not been built to withstand the power of a hurricane as strong as Katrina. Many of them had cracked and broken, letting water crash through into the city. Everything was underwater.

Within minutes, the water in our house was up to our waists. Mom grabbed our dog, Charlie, and Lisa picked up Sugar, our cat.

▲ *Levees are built to help contain water during a flood. Many of the levees around New Orleans failed during Hurricane Katrina.*

▲ *Responders used helicopters and boats to rescue those in danger.*

I took some water bottles from the kitchen, and all of us headed upstairs. In less than an hour, the water was on the second floor, so Mom told us to climb to the attic. And that's where we had been ever since.

The nights were the hardest. The water had risen into the attic and smelled terrible. There was nowhere comfortable to sleep. There was no bathroom. None of us knew what to do to get help. We watched our neighbors climb out on their roofs and get hoisted up by Coast Guard officers, who kept coming by in helicopters. Our attic had only tiny windows, not large enough to climb out of. Whenever a

▲ *More than 5,600 U.S. Coast Guard officers were part of the Hurricane Katrina rescue.*

▲ *The Superdome stadium in New Orleans served as a shelter for people who did not evacuate before Hurricane Katrina.*

helicopter came by, we stuck our hands out of the attic vent and screamed, hoping they would hear and see us. So far, they hadn't.

Lisa and I were dozing when suddenly Charlie began barking loudly. I heard a helicopter. It had come by to get the Fishers, our next-door neighbors. Charlie barked and barked and suddenly there was a pounding on the roof.

"Anyone in there?" someone shouted. I banged on the wall, and my mom began yelling. Seconds later, we heard the sound of an ax breaking through our roof.

"They're here!" Lisa screamed. "Thanks, Charlie," she added. "Good thing we saved you because you just saved us." We all laughed and hugged each other, waiting for a rescue that was only moments away.

Man's Best Friend

According to a National Guard officer, 30 to 40 percent of the people who refused to leave the flooded areas stayed because they wanted to take care of their pets. Unfortunately, most major disaster plans do not include details for how to help people with their animals. Experts estimated that 250,000 dogs and cats were either **displaced** or died due to the effects of the storm.

Chapter 2

Samuel Redmond

Coast Guard Petty Officer Third Class

I looked at the scene below me and tried to comprehend what was happening. Water was everywhere, and on the rooftop of almost every single house, people were standing or sitting, yelling and waving. Cries of "Help! Please help us!" were everywhere. I glanced at the other men riding in the Jayhawk helicopter with me. Where were we supposed to start?

I had learned about Hurricane Katrina just a day ago. All of us had watched the weather forecasts, and it was clear that this was going to be a very dangerous, history-making storm. It ranked as a category 5 hurricane, and winds were predicted to hit up to

▲ *After the hurricane, it is estimated that about 60,000 people needed to be rescued from flooded homes.*

175 miles (282 kilometers) per hour. It was headed directly for New Orleans, a city that was surrounded by water, including the Mississippi River. Much of the city was below **sea level**, so I knew that meant flooding was a serious threat. Now, looking at a city buried in water, mud, and **debris**, I realized the scope of this storm. I was told that once the levees had broken, the average depth of water throughout the city was an unbelievable 20 feet (6 m). No wonder President Bush had declared a federal state of emergency for the city.

"Watch out for phone and electrical wires," shouted our superior, Pitman, to the chopper pilot. "Redmond, you'll be the first one out, so be ready."

Think About It

▶ Reread this chapter. What were the safety risks that rescuers faced? Provide examples to support your answer.

I hooked myself to a cable, and Pitman lowered it to a family of three waiting on their rooftop. I had trained for months on how to rescue people from mountainsides, tall trees, and sinking ships, but never from the top of a house. When I reached the roof, I said, "Hello! I'm from the Coast Guard, and I'm going to help you out of here." Carefully, each member of the family was loaded into the

▲ Towns on the coasts of Louisiana, Mississippi, and Alabama experienced extreme flooding due to Hurricane Katrina.

helicopter, and we flew off to the Superdome where many of the
survivors were being sheltered.

Hours later, we were still rescuing people as fast as possible. In
some situations, we had to go all the way down to street level, and that
proved to be quite a challenge. It's hard to avoid hitting curbs, fire
hydrants, skateboards, bicycles, trash cans, and fences when they are
all several feet underwater. Each time I stumbled, I was grateful for
my thick boots and my kneepads.

In some places, the only way we could reach people was to use the
axes we carried in each chopper. I tore apart a number of roofs to get to
people trapped in attics. My team carried a stretcher with us for anyone
who was sick or injured. By the end of the day, we had been joined by

firefighters and police officers, as well as people from the Army, Navy, and National Guard. A number of survivors from New Orleans also grabbed their boats to help search for anyone at the water level.

The water was truly awful. It was full of waste, oil, rotting food, and trash. Trees were downed everywhere, bridges were out, and train tracks were blocked with debris. I heard about a number of people who tried to leave New Orleans by foot, but when they attempted to cross a bridge, armed police officers turned them back. I shook my head. I was sure that this city would soon run out of safe places for this many displaced people!

▲ *Those seeking shelter at the Superdome endured very difficult conditions.*

▲ *The rescue effort took many days, and restoring damaged areas took even longer.*

"Petty Officer Redmond," shouted Pitman as we were flying back to headquarters for some much-needed rest. "Good work today! We saved a lot of people."

I nodded my thanks, but when I crawled into bed that night, all I could picture was the hundreds of people still waiting for rescue.

Hurricane Katrina's Numbers

People killed in Hurricane Katrina	1,836
Average depth of water in New Orleans	20 feet (6 m)
People without electrical power	2.7 million
People lodged in the Superdome	25,000
Homes destroyed in the hurricane	300,000
Vehicles wrecked in the hurricane	200,000
People rescued by the Coast Guard	33,545

Chapter 3

Tamako Lee

California Student

"Hey, Tamako, want to buy one of my handmade duct tape wallets?" asked Lindsey. "I'm using the money to help the school band order new instruments." I shook my head. I didn't mean to be unfriendly, but I was still too upset over what I heard on the news this morning about New Orleans to think about anything else.

"All right, class, let's settle down," said Mrs. Curtis. I sat down at my desk. I hoped Mrs. Curtis would talk about Hurricane Katrina once she finished taking attendance. Just then, I felt someone tap me on the shoulder. "Hey," whispered Leroy, "don't forget to tell

▲ *Hurricane Katrina and its aftermath were national and international news.*

Analyze This

▶ How is the perspective of Tamako and her
friends different from that of Philip and other
kids in New Orleans? How are they similar?

your parents about the car wash my Boy Scout troop is hosting
tonight! You promised."

I nodded. Leroy had been reminding me about his fund-raiser for
more than a week now.

"Before we get started today," Mrs. Curtis began, "I wanted to
point out what is happening in Louisiana right now. One of history's
biggest storms is hitting the state, especially in New Orleans.
Thousands of people are staying in shelters, and more than a
million have left the city. Winds are blowing more than 125 miles
(201 km) per hour, and now the city's levees have broken, and the
city is flooding."

I raised my hand. "Isn't there something we can do to help these
people?" I asked.

▲ This photo shows a shelter in Texas for those affected by Hurricane Katrina. People and organizations across the country wanted to help.

"That is a good question, Tamako. Why don't we all think about what we can do to help the people of New Orleans? Bring your ideas to class tomorrow."

At lunch, I talked with my best friends about Katrina. We brainstormed some possible ideas of ways to help the city's **residents**. Melanie suggested sending them bottled water. Keira thought we should crochet blankets for everyone. Marcus thought we should send them encouraging notes and cards.

"Hey guys, are you coming to the spaghetti dinner tomorrow night?" asked Tonia. "Everyone is going to be there!"

Oops! I had completely forgotten about the community dinner. I was glad Tonia reminded me. My family and I went every year, and it was always fun.

That night at dinner, I talked to my parents about what was happening in New Orleans. "I am trying to come up with a great way to help the people there, but nothing seems quite right yet," I said. "The Red Cross is already sending water, crocheting blankets will take too long, and I doubt their mail system will be working for weeks or months. Maybe I could raise some money. . . ." My voice trailed off as I suddenly had a great idea.

▲ *The American Red Cross is a charity organization that provides relief to people affected by disaster.*

Second Source

▶ Find a second source that describes what life was like for the people staying in the city's Superdome. How does that information compare to the information in this source?

The next morning in Mrs. Curtis's class, I was the first person to raise my hand when my teacher asked for ideas. "I think sending money is the best thing we can do for the people in New Orleans," I said, "because they can use it wherever they need it most. I think we can do it quickly, too. Lindsey, Leroy, and Tonia"—I paused to point at each of them—"how about we pool what you've earned with your wallets, car washes, and spaghetti dinners and send that to Louisiana? We can add the money in our classroom coin jar, too. What do you think?"

"I think that is a terrific start, Tamako," said Mrs. Curtis. "I will talk to the rest of the staff and make some calls."

As we all got out our history textbooks, Lindsey turned around to whisper to me. "Here!" she said, handing me one of her colorful wallets. "Now you'll have something to put the money in before you send it."

Help in Times of Need

Following Hurricane Katrina, more than 90 countries offered to help the people of New Orleans. Bangladesh pledged $1 million. Thailand offered to send 60 doctors and nurses to help the injured and sick. Kuwait, Qatar, and the United Arab Emirates sent large donations, while Germany sent high-speed pumps to help reduce the amount of floodwater in the city. The Netherlands sent experts on levee construction.

Look, Look Again

This photo shows New Orleans residents being rescued by military helicopter in the aftermath of Hurricane Katrina. Use the photo to answer the questions below:

1. How would someone who had waited days for rescue after Hurricane Katrina react to this photo? Why?

2. How would a rescue worker describe this photo to a friend?

3. What questions might someone who hadn't experienced Hurricane Katrina firsthand have about this photo?

Glossary

debris (duh-BREE) fragments of something that has been destroyed

displaced (dis-PLAYSD) moved out of its usual place

evacuation (ih-vak-yoo-AY-shuhn) the process of moving people to safety

levees (LEV-eez) artificial walls made of earth or gravel and built beside a river

residents (REZ-ih-duhnts) people who live in a place

sea level (SEE LEV-uhl) the average height of the ocean's surface, used as a starting point from which to measure the height of another place

Learn More

Further Reading

Benoit, Peter. *Hurricane Katrina*. New York: Children's Press, 2012.

Brown, Don. *Drowned City: Hurricane Katrina and New Orleans*. New York: Houghton Mifflin Harcourt, 2015.

Hoena, Blake. *Hurricane Katrina: An Interactive Modern History Adventure*. Mankato, MN: Capstone Press, 2014.

Koontz, Robin. *What Was Hurricane Katrina?* New York: Grosset & Dunlap, 2015.

Pratt, Mary. *Hurricane Katrina and the Flooding of New Orleans: A Cause-and-Effect Investigation*. Minneapolis: Lerner Publications, 2017.

Tarshis, Lauren. *I Survived Hurricane Katrina, 2005*. New York: Scholastic Books, 2011.

Zullo, Allan. *Heroes of Hurricane Katrina*. New York: Scholastic Books, 2015.

Web Sites

Facts for Kids—Hurricane Katrina Facts for Kids
http://factsforkids.net/hurricane-katrina-facts-for-kids

Scholastic News—Remembering Hurricane Katrina
http://magazines.scholastic.com/kids-press/news/2015/08/Remembering-Hurricane-Katrina

Index

About the Author

Tamra Orr recalls watching the news reports about Hurricane Katrina and staying in close touch with a friend who lived in the area. She is the author of hundreds of books for readers of all ages. She lives in the Pacific Northwest with her family and spends all of her free time writing letters, reading books, and going camping. She graduated from Ball State University with a degree in English and education, and believes she has the best job in the world. It gives her the chance to keep learning all about the world and the people in it.